I0178068

ADMINISTRATIVE PROFESSIONALS WHO LEAD

CARLOS BUTLER HARLEM

&

LILETTA HARLEM

Copyright © 2023 by Carlos Butler Harlem and Liletta Harlem

All rights reserved.

No part of this publication may be reproduced, stored in a retrieval system, or transmitted in any form or by any means, electronic, mechanical, scanning, recording, photocopying, or otherwise, without the prior written permission of the authors.

Limit of Liability/Disclaimer of Warranty: This publication is designed to provide accurate and authoritative information regarding the subject matter covered. It is sold with the understanding that neither the author nor the publisher is engaged in rendering legal, investment, accounting, or other professional services. While the publisher and author have used their best efforts in preparing this book, they make no representations or warranties with respect to the accuracy or completeness of the contents of this book and specifically disclaim any implied warranties of merchantability or fitness for a particular purpose. No warranty may be created or extended by sales representatives or written sales materials. The advice and strategies contained herein may not be suitable for your situation. You should consult with a professional when appropriate. Neither the publisher nor the author shall be liable for any loss of profit or any other commercial damages, including but not limited to special, incidental, consequential, personal, or other damages.

Administrative Professionals Who Lead

By Carlos Butler Harlem & Liletta Harlem

Paperback ISBN: ISBN: 978-1-7348617-6-1

Cover design by Brittany Veney

Printed in the United States of America

Carlos Butler Harlem and Liletta Harlem

www.businesscrossingnetwork.com

Contents

Introduction

Welcome to this guidebook, where the journey to becoming an exceptional administrative professional begins! Whether you're here to enhance your administrative skills or aspire to lead with excellence, you've recognized the pivotal role that solid administrative abilities play in organizational success.

Administrative skills are the backbone of streamlined business processes. In any thriving company or organization, individuals with adept administrative skills are essential contributors. These skills extend beyond merely handling office tasks; they encompass effective teamwork, meticulous documentation, and the ability to innovate processes for the betterment of customers, employees, and stakeholders.

Working with a team demands strong administrative skills to meet their needs, listen to their requirements, and navigate challenges efficiently. Imagine trying to operate a well-oiled machine without someone on the team possessing these vital skills—it's simply inconceivable.

You might be wondering, "What defines an administrative professional?" There are numerous descriptions, but in essence, it involves handling diverse responsibilities such as office tasks, scheduling support, travel arrangements, phone call screening, report generation, and more. Regardless of the industry or whether you run your own business, these responsibilities are integral to a well-functioning organization.

Many businesses face challenges because their innovators lack these fundamental administrative skills, resulting in a loss of trust from customers and clients.

So, what can you expect from this book? It's designed to provide you with practical tips, valuable lessons, and actionable steps to master professionalism, leadership, and elevate your administrative skills to thrive as a successful entrepreneur. To make your learning journey simple and straightforward, we've distilled the keys to success into five steps:

Step 1: Self Awareness

Step 2: Know Your Audience! Everyone is your ally

Step 3: Communication Is Key

Step 4: Forward Thinking

Step 5: You Are The CEO

Are you ready to learn?

Before we dive in, let's establish that the foundation of an administrative professional is rooted in excellent customer service. Your role is to access information, convert it to knowledge, and communicate that knowledge to customers in a way that adds value. Moreover, viewing everyone as your customer, whether an executive or a peer, lays a strong foundation for becoming a highly valued administrative professional.

Now, let's embark on this transformative journey together!

CHAPTER 1

Self-Awareness

Self-Awareness is the cornerstone of successful leadership. Understanding oneself, or self-awareness, is the linchpin that sets the stage for effective leadership. But what does self-awareness entail? Simply put, it's the ability to focus on your actions, thoughts, and emotions, evaluating how they align or deviate from your internal standards.

Now, let's explore how to enhance your self-awareness through practical steps:

Keep an Open Mind: Regulating your emotions allows you to be attuned to others' feelings. Cultivate curiosity about new people and the diverse perspectives they bring.

Mind Your Strengths and Weaknesses: Self-aware individuals grasp their strengths and weaknesses, enabling them to work from a place of understanding. Recognize when to seek assistance and when to tackle situations independently.

Stay Focused: Train yourself to maintain focus over extended periods, resisting the pull of social media, emails, or other minor distractions.

Set Boundaries: Establish firm limits. Be warm yet assertive, saying no when necessary. Uphold the integrity of your goals by enforcing boundaries, even if it means walking away from a situation.

Know Your Emotional Triggers: Identify your emotions as they arise. Rather than repressing or denying them, navigate and process them before engaging with others.

Practice Self-Discipline: Strive for discipline in all aspects of your life, as it forms the bedrock of strong leadership.

Consider the Impact of Your Actions: Acknowledge not only your emotions but also how your actions affect those around you. Being considerate of others helps navigate challenging situations.

Apologize When Necessary: Mistakes are inevitable, but self-awareness empowers you to recognize when apologies are warranted. Adopting an apologetic mindset, even when not directly responsible, strengthens your reputation as an administrative leader.

Ask for Feedback: While self-awareness involves understanding oneself independently, seeking feedback requires courage. It acknowledges natural biases and provides a more objective perspective. Don't assume everything is okay because no one has spoken up—seek feedback proactively.

Try the following exercise to deepen your self-awareness. Answer the following questions to the best of your ability.

- I am strong in these areas:

- I struggle with:

- The most stressful part of my day is:

- I'd like some help with:

- When I need help, I'm comfortable asking for it in the following ways:

- When I'm frustrated, I usually feel better when I:

- When I make a mistake, the first thing I do is:

Let's shift our focus to a crucial aspect of self-awareness: reflecting on your answers. This step involves a thoughtful examination of your responses to various situations and scenarios. Take a moment to review them and gauge how well they align with your internal standards.

But don't stop there; invite a trusted friend or advisor into the process. Share your reflections with them and encourage an open conversation. Consider their perspective on how they perceive your responses and compare it with your own assessment.

Here's how you can navigate this step:

1. Reflect on Your Answers: Take the time to revisit your responses. Are they in harmony with your internal standards and the person you strive to be?

2. Seek an External Perspective: Enlist the help of a trusted friend or advisor. Share your reflections with them and inquire about their thoughts on your answers.

3. Compare Perspectives: Compare your own assessment with the external perspective. Identify areas of alignment and potential discrepancies.

4. Engage in Conversation: Initiate a conversation with your trusted confidant. Discuss the reasons behind any disparities in perception. This dialogue can provide valuable insights into your self-awareness journey.

5. Embrace Constructive Feedback: Be open to constructive feedback. It's an opportunity for growth and a deeper understanding of yourself.

This reflective process, coupled with external input, serves as a powerful tool for honing your self-awareness.

My Notes

My Notes

CHAPTER 2

Know the Audience! Everyone is your ally

⌒✍⌒

L et's delve into the realm of building professional allies—a vital endeavor for career growth and success. Establishing connections in your industry starts with effective networking strategies. Attending industry events, becoming part of professional organizations, and connecting with like-minded individuals on business platforms. The key is to foster genuine relationships grounded in mutual respect and shared objectives. Helping on projects and seeking collaborative opportunities strengthens these connections. Always uphold professionalism and integrity in your interactions to nurture lasting alliances.

Building professional allies is a continuous journey that demands patience and dedication. Here are proven tips to fortify your professional network:

Be Authentic: Genuine interactions matter. Avoid pretending to be someone you're not or exaggerating your experience, as sincerity is easily recognized.

Follow Up: After networking events or online encounters, take the time to follow up. Send a brief email expressing gratitude for their time and convey your interest in maintaining contact.

Give Back: Contribute to your community or industry through volunteer work or speaking engagements. This not only helps others but also enhances your visibility and credibility.

Seek Mentorship: Join a mentorship program or find a mentor independently. Having a trusted advisor offers invaluable guidance and support throughout your career.

Attend Industry Events: Regularly participate in industry events and conferences to meet new people, stay informed about industry trends, and foster connections.

Utilize Social Media: Leverage social media platforms to connect with professionals. Share insightful content, engage in discussions, and follow up with online connections to cultivate lasting relationships.

Join Professional Associations: Become a part of professional associations or groups related to your field for access to valuable resources, networking opportunities, and potential job leads.

Be Proactive: Take initiative in networking. Reach out to individuals you admire or respect in your industry, proposing coffee meetings or phone chats.

Show Respect: Uphold respect and courtesy in your interactions. Treat others as you wish to be treated, recognizing that building strong professional relationships requires time and effort.

Remember, building relationships is an investment with significant returns. By nurturing your professional network, you gain access to opportunities, knowledge, and career advancement.

Transitioning to supporting others in business, it's not just about receiving but also giving. Mentorship, knowledge sharing, networking, feedback, and collaboration are ways to contribute to the success of others. Celebrate achievements and provide encouragement during challenging times.

Here are additional suggestions to support others in business:

Provide Learning Opportunities: Organize workshops or training sessions to help others develop new skills, showcasing your commitment to their success.

Offer Introductions: Facilitate connections by introducing individuals to potential clients, partners, or investors, expanding their network.

Share Your Platform: If you have a blog, podcast, or a significant social media following, feature someone else's work or promote their business to your audience, helping them gain exposure.

Supporting others is not just altruistic; it's a mutually beneficial endeavor. Strengthening relationships and cultivating a network of trusted peers can lead to future opportunities and collaborations. It's a journey worth taking for personal and professional growth.

My Notes

My Notes

CHAPTER 3

Communication Is Key

In the realm of leadership, thinking like a leader is synonymous with effective communication. It's not just about conveying ideas; it's about creating a framework for success. When leaders communicate well, they articulate their vision, goals, and expectations clearly, fostering trust and transparency within the team. This, in turn, lays the foundation for better relationships and a positive work environment.

But it goes beyond that. Effective communication serves various purposes, becoming the linchpin for a well-functioning team.

Conflict Resolution:

When conflicts arise, open communication becomes the linchpin for timely and effective resolution.

Motivation:

A leader's clear communication of vision and goals inspires team members, aligning them towards a common objective and driving success.

Feedback:

Regular communication and feedback pave the way for team members to understand their strengths and weaknesses, fostering personal and professional growth.

Innovation:

Open communication channels fuel creativity and idea-sharing, propelling innovation, and progress.

Building Trust:

Transparent communication builds trust between leaders and team members, enhancing engagement and commitment.

Preventing Misunderstandings:

Clear communication is the antidote to workplace misunderstandings and mistakes. When everyone understands their roles and responsibilities, things are less likely to go awry.

Fostering a Culture of Respect:

Effective communication helps leaders cultivate a culture of respect. When leaders communicate clearly and respectfully, they set the tone for others to follow.

Encouraging Collaboration:

Communication is the key to effective collaboration. When team members communicate openly and honestly, they can work together seamlessly to achieve their goals.

In essence, effective communication is the lifeline for administrative leaders aiming to create a positive and productive work environment. Prioritizing communication as a cornerstone of leadership enables administrative professionals to not only lead but to guide their team towards thriving and succeeding. It's a holistic approach that transforms communication from a mere tool to an integral part of leadership prowess.

Questions you can ask yourself to determine if you have good communication skills

- Do I listen actively and attentively to others?
- Do I express my ideas clearly and effectively?
- Am I able to adjust my communication style to fit different situations and audiences?
- Do I ask thoughtful questions to clarify understanding and show interest?
- Am I mindful of nonverbal cues and body language?
- Do I give constructive feedback and receive criticism well?
- Can I navigate conflicts and difficult conversations with respect and professionalism?

- Do I use appropriate language and tone in different contexts?

- Am I able to persuade and influence others in a positive way?

- Do I foster open and honest communication in my relationships and interactions?

Answering these questions can help you assess your communication skills and identify areas for improvement.

Below are a few additional tips to enhance your communication skills:

- Practice active listening by paying attention to what others are saying, asking questions to clarify their message, and providing feedback to show that you understand.

- Use clear and concise language to express your thoughts and ideas. Avoid using jargon or technical language that may be difficult for others to understand.

- Adapt your communication style to match the situation and audience. For example, you may need to use a more formal tone in a professional setting or use simple language when communicating with someone who has limited knowledge on the topic.

- Be mindful of your nonverbal cues, such as facial expressions, gestures, and tone of voice. These cues can convey a lot of information and impact how your message is received.

- Provide constructive feedback by focusing on specific behaviors or actions rather than attacking someone's character. When receiving criticism, try to stay open-minded and use it as an opportunity to learn and grow.

- When navigating conflicts or difficult conversations, focus on finding a solution rather than assigning blame. Use active listening and empathy to understand the other person's perspective.

- Use appropriate language and tone depending on the context. For example, you may need to adjust your language when speaking with someone from a different cultural background or when discussing sensitive topics.

- Use persuasion and influence in a positive way by focusing on the benefits and providing evidence to support your argument.

- Foster open and honest communication in your relationships by being transparent, respectful, and empathetic. Encourage others to share their thoughts and ideas and listen actively to their feedback.

By implementing these tips and regularly assessing and improving your communication skills, you can become a more effective communicator and enhance your personal and professional relationships.

Review the following diagram and do a bit of self-reflection. Can you see yourself in the scenario? How would you have handled the situation?

Take time to write down your thoughts in the notes section.

Jessica is working late to finish a project and receives an email about an employee. The employee made a critical mistake in front of stakeholders, Jessica is extremely frustrated!

Jessica's initial response is to write a very long and detailed email to the employee, explaining what he did wrong and how to fix his mistake.

Jessica soon remembers that she is working on her effective and appropriate communication. She realizes that for her communication to be appropriate and reach the desired result, she should NOT answer while her emotions are high, and at an inappropriate time.

The next morning, after getting some rest, Jessica decides that a video meeting would work much better than an email. This allows Jessica to read facial expressions and tone of voice and adjust accordingly, ensuring that her message is effective.

My Notes

My Notes

CHAPTER 4

Forward Thinking

Being a strong administrative professional requires that you be a forward-thinking leader. Forward-thinking leaders must make sound decisions and carry out present-day business tasks strategically while also focusing on success down the road. They must be in touch with their team, their organization, and the rapidly changing modern business landscape. Take risks and experiment.

A few ways to think ahead:

- Have several options and pathways to achieve a goal. As an individual and for the team, this forward-thinking trait is key to good leadership.

- Learn from the past.

- Avoid a competitive mindset. Instead, see others in your field as collaborators and realize that the marketplace allows competitors to all win because consumers will always have unique needs and preferences.

- Find the balance between being overly critical and reasonably critical. The goal is not to put yourself down, but to see professional gaps and weaknesses and correct them.

- Thinking ahead can create new opportunities you were not aware of. But this also requires you to knock on the doors you want to open. You must find courage in corners you never knew existed and be prepared for any opportunity.

- Thinking ahead will help you reach your goals.

Here are some methods to increase your ability to anticipate the future.

- Understand your 'why.'

- Absorb knowledge from a wide range of sources and do not forget to take in what people from other fields have to say.

- Have courage.

- Embody & embrace creative thinking.

- Think critically and be willing to explore other options from outside your experience, belief, and value set.

Problem Solving Tips

- Focus on the problem itself, not on what you think is causing it.

- Describe the problem objectively and clearly.

- Decide on the type of problem you are dealing with before you attempt to solve it.

- Most problems have multiple solutions. Be willing to review and adjust in order find the best solution.

- Involve the key stakeholders right from the beginning and then continuously throughout the process.

- Stay away from blaming someone for the problem. Identifying the source of the problem doesn't fix it.

- Remember that often, fixing one part of the problem can drastically impact another area. Be aware of this balance and weigh all options.

My Notes

My Notes

CHAPTER 5

You Are The CEO

Understanding what it truly means to be a CEO is the key to adopting a CEO mindset within any organization. The Chief Executive Officer, or CEO, holds the highest executive position, steering the ship by making critical corporate decisions, managing resources, and overseeing overall operations. In essence, CEOs play a pivotal role in shaping the company's trajectory and success.

For one to think like a CEO, it's crucial to grasp the multifaceted responsibilities inherent in the role. CEOs must strike a delicate balance, considering the needs of various stakeholders—employees, customers, shareholders, and the broader community. This demands a unique blend of leadership skills, strategic thinking, and business acumen.

Thinking like a CEO is a mindset shift where you take ownership of your role. It involves assuming responsibility for assigned tasks, proactively seeking ways to enhance processes and outcomes, and being accountable for your actions and decisions. This mindset embodies proactivity, reliability, and unwavering commitment to achieving goals and contributing to team and organizational success.

With a CEO mindset, you recognize the weight of your role, even when others falter. It's about accepting consequences, promptly addressing issues, and taking decisive action to prevent future failures. This proactive approach ensures that you safeguard the image and reputation of your business or product—the essence of your brand.

Your brand is more than a logo; it's the image and reputation your business conveys to the world. Understanding its value and investing in its development and maintenance are vital. This entails consistent messaging, visual branding, and a focus on delivering exceptional customer experiences.

In essence, thinking like a CEO transcends mere job responsibilities. It's a commitment to excellence, a proactive mindset, and a deep understanding of the brand's significance in setting your business apart, fostering customer loyalty, building trust, and ultimately driving increased revenue.

Thinking like a CEO as an administrative professional goes hand in hand with maintaining a strong brand. Let's explore how you can elevate your brand identity within this context:

Creating a Brand Style Guide: A crucial step in brand maintenance is developing a comprehensive brand style guide. This guide delineates key elements such as the color palette, typography, logo usage, and tone of voice. With these guidelines in place, consistency becomes the cornerstone of all marketing materials, social media posts, and communications, ensuring alignment with your brand identity.

Positive Customer Experience: As an administrative professional, you play a pivotal role in shaping the customer experience. Building a seamless and user-friendly website, providing excellent customer service, and delivering high-quality products or services contribute to a positive customer experience. Consistently exceeding expectations not only fosters customer loyalty but also fuels brand awareness through word-of-mouth recommendations.

Regular Monitoring and Analysis: Keep a vigilant eye on your brand's performance by monitoring various metrics. Track social media engagement, customer feedback, and sales data to gauge how your brand is perceived in the market. This ongoing analysis empowers you to make informed decisions about future marketing strategies and brand development initiatives.

By intertwining these brand-maintenance strategies with your CEO mindset, you elevate your role as an administrative professional. You become a custodian of the brand, ensuring that every interaction, communication, and customer touchpoint aligns seamlessly with the established brand identity. This holistic approach not only strengthens the brand but also reinforces your commitment to excellence in your administrative role.

To further strengthen your brand identity, here are some additional tips to consider:

- Develop a brand story that resonates with your target audience. This can be achieved by highlighting your brand's values, mission, and unique selling proposition.

- Take advantage of visual content to reinforce your brand identity. This can include creating custom graphics, videos, and other visual assets that align with your brand's guidelines.

- Leverage influencer marketing to expand your reach and build credibility. This involves partnering with individuals who have a large following and can promote your brand to their audience.

- Engage with your audience on social media by responding to comments, sharing user-generated content, and hosting giveaways to increase engagement.

- Continuously evolve your brand by staying up to date with industry trends and adapting to changes in your target audience's preferences and behaviors. This can involve conducting regular market research and analyzing your competition.

Overall, investing in your brand's development and maintenance can have a significant impact on your business's success. By creating a strong brand identity and providing a positive customer experience, you can build a loyal customer base and stand out in a crowded marketplace.

Another focus of a CEO is to ensure professionalism. Professionalism is the conduct, behavior, and attitude expected of someone in a particular profession or workplace. It is characterized by competence, integrity, respect, and adherence to ethical standards. Professionalism involves a commitment to high-quality work, effective communication, and collaboration with others. It is important for building trust, establishing credibility, and achieving success in one's career.

In addition to the traits and qualities mentioned, professionalism also includes some other key aspects that define a person's professional conduct. Some of these are:

- Being punctual, meeting deadlines, and respecting others' time are all important aspects of professionalism. It shows that you are dependable and value other people's schedules.

- Dressing professionally is important as it helps to create a positive impression on others. Wearing appropriate clothing also shows that you respect the work environment and take your job seriously.

- Taking responsibility for one's actions and decisions is an important aspect of professionalism. It shows that you are willing to learn from your mistakes, take corrective action, and improve your performance.

- Professionals are expected to keep themselves updated with the latest developments in their field. This involves continuous learning, attending workshops and seminars, and staying informed about industry trends.

Professionals must possess excellent communication skills to be able to clearly articulate their ideas, listen actively, and provide constructive feedback. Effective communication skills help in building strong relationships with colleagues, clients, and stakeholders, which is crucial for success in any profession.

They are also expected to uphold ethical standards and maintain integrity in all their interactions. They should always act in the best interest of their clients or organization, avoid conflicts of interest, and ensure that their actions are legal and ethical.

Being adaptable is important in today's dynamic work environment. Professionals should be able to adapt to changes, learn new skills, take on new responsibilities, and handle new challenges with ease. This shows that they are versatile and able to thrive in any situation.

Teamwork: Professionals should be able to work collaboratively with others, contribute to team goals, and support their colleagues. This includes being respectful, open-minded, and willing to compromise to achieve common objectives. Strong teamwork skills can help in building a positive work environment and improving overall productivity.

By demonstrating these qualities and behaviors consistently, you can establish yourself as a professional and build trust and respect with your colleagues and clients.

My Notes

My Notes

Conclusion

In the dynamic landscape of administrative leadership, adopting a CEO mindset and maintaining a strong brand identity emerge as pivotal elements for success. Thinking like a CEO transcends conventional roles, urging professionals to take ownership, foster proactive approaches, and ensure accountability. This mindset becomes a driving force for effective communication, conflict resolution, and the creation of a positive work environment.

Simultaneously, the responsibility extends to nurturing and safeguarding the brand identity. Administrative professionals, as leaders, become stewards of the brand, utilizing style guides for consistency, championing positive customer experiences, and vigilantly monitoring brand performance.

By embracing this mindset and safeguarding the brand identity, administrative professionals become architects of success, contributing not only to their teams' thriving environments but also to the legacy of the organizations they serve. This integrated approach sets the stage for continuous growth, resilience, and a powerful impact in the ever-evolving landscape of professional leadership.

Whether you are new in the administrative field, embarking on a role as a virtual administrative professional, or looking to refresh your skills, this book is a resource for you to use for your growth.

The next few pages are filled with additional terms, resources, and updates to continue to assist you with your goal of being an Administrative Professional who Leads!

Important Terms

Review the following important terms that will help you become more effective in your role as an administrative professional.

Leadership

Good leadership involves a combination of traits and skills, such as effective communication, problem-solving, empathy, integrity, accountability, and the ability to inspire and motivate others. Some examples of good leadership include leading by example, leading with a clear vision, promoting teamwork and collaboration, and being adaptable and open to change. Additionally, good leaders prioritize the well-being and growth of their team members, and they seek to develop their own leadership skills through continuous learning and feedback.

It is important to note that good leadership is not a one-size-fits-all approach. Different situations may require different leadership styles and strategies. For instance, a crisis may require a leader to make quick decisions and take charge, while a long-term project may benefit from a more collaborative and participatory leadership approach.

In addition, good leaders understand the importance of diversity and inclusion in the workplace. They recognize the unique strengths and perspectives that each team member brings to the table and create an environment where everyone feels valued and respected. This not only fosters a positive work culture, but also leads to better decision-making and creativity.

Moreover, good leaders recognize the impact of their actions and decisions on their team and the organization. They take responsibility for their mistakes and failures and work to make things right. They also celebrate their team's successes and give credit where credit is due.

Overall, good leadership is a continuous process of self-reflection, growth, and development. It requires a combination of skills, traits, and strategies that are tailored to the situation at hand, and a commitment to creating a positive and inclusive work environment.

Organization

Good organization refers to the practice of arranging information or resources in a logical and efficient manner. This can apply to physical objects, digital files, or even schedules and plans. Benefits of good organization include increased productivity, reduced stress, and easier access to important information.

When it comes to organizing physical objects, it's important to consider the layout of the space. Here are some tips to help you get started:

- Use storage containers or shelves to keep items off the ground and in a designated space.
- Label containers so that you can easily identify what is inside.
- Group similar items together to make them easier to locate.
- Consider the frequency of use when deciding where to store items - frequently used items should be easily accessible.

In terms of digital organization, there are many tools available to help you keep track of files and information.

Try these suggestions:

- Use a naming convention that makes sense to you and is consistent across all files.
- Create folders to keep related files together.
- Use tags or keywords to make searching for specific files easier.
- Regularly delete or archive outdated files to prevent clutter.

Overall, good organization can have a significant impact on your productivity and well-being. By taking the time to arrange your physical and digital spaces in a logical and efficient manner, you can reduce stress and increase your ability to focus on the task at hand.

Time Management

Time management refers to the practice of organizing and planning how much time is spent on various activities to maximize productivity and efficiency. It involves setting goals, prioritizing tasks, and avoiding distractions to make the most of available time. Effective time management can help reduce stress, increase productivity, and improve overall quality of life.

In today's fast-paced world, time management has become an essential skill for both personal and professional success. Here are some tips to help you improve your time management skills:

- Make a to-do list: Writing down all the tasks you need to accomplish in a day can help you stay organized and focused. Prioritize tasks based on their importance and deadline.

- Use a calendar: A calendar can help you keep track of important dates, deadlines, and appointments. You can use a physical calendar or a digital one, whichever works best for you.

- Avoid multitasking: Contrary to popular belief, multitasking can decrease productivity and increase stress. Instead, focus on one task at a time and give it your full attention.

- Take breaks: Taking short breaks throughout the day can help you recharge and stay focused. Use your breaks to stretch, go for a walk, or do something that relaxes you.

- Minimize distractions: Distractions such as social media, email notifications, and phone calls can disrupt your workflow. Try to minimize these distractions by turning off notifications or setting aside specific times to check them.

Improving your time management skills can have a significant impact on your productivity and overall well-being. Here are some additional tips to help you make the most of your time:

- Set realistic goals: When setting goals, make sure they are realistic and achievable within the given time frame. This will help you avoid feeling overwhelmed and stressed.

- Prioritize self-care: Taking care of yourself is essential for optimal productivity. Make sure to prioritize self-care activities such as exercise, meditation, or spending time with loved ones.

- Learn to delegate: Delegating tasks to others can help you free up time and focus on more important tasks. When delegating, make sure to choose the right person for the job and provide clear instructions.

- Schedule buffer time: Scheduling buffer time between tasks or meetings can help you avoid running late or feeling rushed. This will also give you time to reflect on the previous task and prepare for the next one.

- Review your progress: Regularly reviewing your progress can help you stay on track and make necessary adjustments to your time management strategies. Take time to reflect on what worked well and what could be improved upon.

Remember, effective time management takes practice and patience. By implementing these tips, you can become more productive, reduce stress, and improve your overall quality of life.

Communication

Good communication refers to the exchange of information between individuals or groups in a clear, effective, and respectful manner. It involves active listening, effective speaking, and understanding the context of the message being conveyed. Good communication skills are essential in personal and professional relationships. Effective communication skills can lead to numerous benefits in both personal and professional settings. Here are some additional points to consider:

- In the workplace, good communication can increase productivity, improve teamwork, and reduce misunderstandings that can lead to errors or conflicts.

- Active listening is a critical component of effective communication. It involves paying attention to what the other person is saying, asking questions to clarify any doubts, and providing feedback to ensure that the message is understood correctly.

- Effective speaking involves using clear and concise language, avoiding jargon or technical terms that the listener may not understand, and adapting the message to the audience's level of understanding.

- Understanding the context of the message is also essential. It involves considering the cultural, social, and emotional factors that can influence how the message is received and interpreted.

- Good communication skills can also improve personal relationships by fostering empathy, understanding, and mutual respect.

- To improve your communication skills, you can practice active listening, seek feedback from others, and learn to adapt your communication style to different situations.

"People Person"

The phrase "being a people person" typically refers to someone who is sociable, outgoing, and enjoys interacting with others.

Being a people person can have many benefits, including the ability to network effectively, develop meaningful relationships, and build a strong sense of community. People who possess this trait tend to excel in careers that involve frequent interactions with others, such as sales, customer service, and public relations. They are often skilled at reading and understanding social cues, which can help them navigate complex social situations and build rapport with others.

If you are not naturally a people person, there are still ways to develop this skill. For example, you can practice active listening by paying attention to what others are saying and asking thoughtful questions. You can also show empathy by putting yourself in others' shoes and trying to understand their perspectives. Seeking out social opportunities, such as joining clubs or attending events, can also help you build your confidence and improve your social skills. With time and effort, anyone can become a people person and enjoy the many benefits that come with it.

Humility

Humility is the quality of being humble and not overly proud or arrogant. It involves recognizing one's own limitations and imperfections and being open to learning from others. In many cultures, humility is considered a desirable trait and is often associated with wisdom, compassion, and inner strength.

Humility is an important quality in many aspects of life, including personal relationships, the workplace, and leadership positions. In the workplace, humility can lead to better collaboration and teamwork. When we are open to learning from others, we can benefit from their expertise and perspectives, and work together more effectively towards common goals.

In leadership positions, humility can inspire trust and respect from others. A humble leader is more likely to listen to feedback and ideas from their team, and to make decisions that prioritize the greater good rather than their own ego.

Overall, practicing humility can help us to be more compassionate, understanding, and effective in our interactions with others.

Administrative Tips

U se and save the following tips as handy resources for effective administrative leadership! These can be reminders that follow you throughout your administrative journey!

Mailbox Management

Folders and Labels: Create folders in Outlook and labels in Google to categorize emails. Sort messages based on projects, clients, or priority.

Rules and Filters: Set up rules in Outlook and filters in Gmail to automate email organization. Route specific emails to designated folders or apply labels automatically.

Flagging and Star System: Flag important emails in Outlook or use the star system in Gmail to highlight crucial messages. This helps prioritize and find them quickly.

Quick Replies and Templates: Save time with quick replies or templates for commonly sent emails. In Outlook, use Quick Parts, and in Gmail, explore the Canned Responses feature.

Stay on Top of Tasks: Tasks and Reminders: Integrate tasks and reminders with your email. Use

Outlook's To-Do List or Google Tasks to manage assignments directly from your inbox.

Calendar Integration: Connect your email and calendar. Schedule meetings, set reminders, and view appointments seamlessly, enhancing productivity.

Unsubscribe and Filters: Unsubscribe from unnecessary newsletters. Utilize filters in Gmail and the Focused Inbox feature in Outlook to reduce clutter and focus on essential emails.

Archive and Cleanup: Archive emails you've dealt with to keep your inbox clean. Outlook's Archive feature and Gmail's Archive button help declutter without deleting.

Use Search Filters: Master search filters to find emails quickly. In both Outlook and Gmail, learn advanced search operators to refine your search queries.

Keyword Organization: Label emails with relevant keywords for better search results. This makes it easier to locate specific information when needed.

Two-Factor Authentication: Enable two-factor authentication for enhanced security. This adds an extra layer of protection to your email accounts.

Regular Security Checkups: Periodically review security settings and update passwords. Be cautious of phishing emails and avoid clicking on suspicious links.

Explore Updates and Features: Stay informed about new features and updates. Both Outlook and Gmail frequently introduce enhancements to improve user experience.

Keyboard Shortcuts: Learn and use keyboard shortcuts to navigate efficiently. This speeds up your workflow and enhance your overall email management experience.

By following these tips, you can streamline your email management process and maintain a more organized and productive digital workspace.

Craft a Consistent Brand Persona

Ensure that your social media presence reflects a cohesive and professional brand persona. Develop a clear brand voice, style, and messaging that aligns with your business values and objectives. Consistency across platforms establishes credibility and reinforces your brand identity.

Define Your Brand Voice: Clearly outline the tone and style you want your brand to convey. Whether it's formal, casual, friendly, or informative, your brand voice should resonate with your target audience.

Create a Content Strategy: Develop a comprehensive content strategy that aligns with your brand persona. Plan your posts, ensuring a mix of promotional content, industry insights, engaging visuals, and any other content that resonates with your audience.

Use Professional Imagery: Visual content is powerful. Use high-quality images and graphics that are consistent with your brand. Avoid inappropriate or unprofessional visuals that may harm your business reputation.

Be Mindful of Language: Choose your words carefully. Avoid slang, offensive language, or anything that could be misinterpreted. Strive for clarity and professionalism in all written communication.

Respond Professionally: Engage with your audience in a timely and respectful manner. Respond to comments, messages, and mentions with professionalism, even in the face of criticism. Address concerns privately whenever possible.

Educate Your Team: If multiple team members manage your social media accounts, ensure they are well-versed in the brand guidelines and understand the importance of maintaining professionalism online.

Monitor and Adjust: Regularly monitor your social media accounts for feedback, comments, and trends. Use analytics to understand what content resonates best with your audience and adjust your strategy accordingly.

Remember, your social media presence is an extension of your brand. By consistently portraying a professional image, you build trust with your audience and strengthen your business reputation. Strive for Timely and Consistent Responses

Customer Service Communication

Establish clear guidelines for response times based on the nature of inquiries. For example, aim to respond to customer inquiries within 24 hours and prioritize urgent matters for immediate attention.

Differentiate Response Times: Recognize that response times may vary depending on the platform and the type of communication. For instance, responses on social media platforms may require quicker turnaround than email inquiries.

Utilize Automation Wisely: Implement automation tools for acknowledging messages or setting expectations about response times. However, use automation judiciously to avoid impersonal interactions and ensure that real-time, personalized responses are still a priority.

Provide Real-time Support: If feasible for your business, offer real-time support through chat or instant messaging. Customers appreciate immediate assistance, especially when facing issues that require quick resolution.

Establish Service Level Agreements (SLAs): Create internal SLAs to formalize response time commitments. This helps your team understand expectations and ensures a consistent level of service across all customer interactions.

Prioritize Urgent Matters: Train your team to identify and prioritize urgent matters. Implement a system that flags and escalates high-priority issues, allowing for swift resolution and preventing potential customer dissatisfaction.

Monitor and Evaluate: Regularly monitor your team's performance in meeting response time targets. Use feedback from customers and analytics data to identify areas for improvement and refine your approach over time.

Communicate Delays Transparently: In cases where a longer response time is unavoidable, communicate transparently with the customer. Set realistic expectations and, if possible, provide interim updates to keep them informed.

Remember, the goal is not just to respond quickly, but to provide thoughtful, helpful, and accurate responses. Consistency in your approach to response times contributes to building trust with your audience and enhances the overall customer experience.

My Notes

My Notes

My Notes

My Notes

My Notes

My Notes

My Notes

My Notes

My Notes

My Notes

www.ingramcontent.com/pod-product-compliance
Lightning Source LLC
Chambersburg PA
CBHW070759050426
42452CB00012B/2403